Joy Mead

WINTER SONG

Poems for our times and occasions

Wintersong

JOY MEAD

Poems for our times and occasions

wild goose
publications www.**ionabooks**.com

First published 2023 by
Wild Goose Publications
Suite 9, Fairfield
1048 Govan Road, Glasgow G51 4XS, Scotland
the publishing division of the Iona Community.
Scottish Charity No. SC003794. Limited Company Reg. No. SC096243.

ISBN 978-1-80432-280-2

Cover artwork © Steve Raw | www.stephenraw.com

Overseas distribution
Australia: Willow Connection Pty Ltd, 1/13 Kell Mather Drive,
Lennox Head NSW 2478
New Zealand: Pleroma, Higginson Street, Otane 4170,
Central Hawkes Bay

Printed by Bell & Bain, Thornliebank, Glasgow

Contents

… the little light
the moth knows
and the fox pauses in …

Silences …

Around the jagged edge of silence:
stories, images … waiting
without pattern.

**

An almost perfect image
of silence:
beneath the tree
empty chairs
placed thoughtfully
in a circle
waiting …

**

He never spoke
of the war.
She knew a little:
thought of sun, fun
and maybe a woman left …
He loved beautiful Sicily
but the Campaign was bloody,
and he found no words
to let into the silent
emptiness of dread.

**

Underneath the talking,
below the conversation,
the unspoken,
the dread,
the silence.

**

On the other side
of silence
is a sea-washed stone
to fit perfectly
into my open hands.
It is what it is.
It holds its question.

**

His face a blank page
    unreadable …
His silence
    unbreakable …
His mind a hidden wonder
    of gathered thoughts …

The boy whose mind
worked differently
loved the silences.
Listened …

**

As a river flows
to its own nothingness
so life takes the words
and gives back silence.

**

My body is silent memory,
of a lifetime
laughing and weeping.

**

I am old in my being
and running out of words.
The caged bird of silence
carried from childhood
still there
waiting to be free …

**

Words written in pencil
disturb the silence
gently.

**

The white froth
of cow parsley
is silence
made visible.

**

The words out there –
somewhere –
ask to be drawn in
to each quiet moment,
to make a fully formed poem,
a story to live by,
a pause on the edge
of silence …

**

It's life-giving, to know stillness
in sacred moments savoured
each time as if the first time:
the play of light
on the surface of water,
the hen harrier's soundless gliding
between us and the open sea,
the fullness of the seed
resting in my hand,
the particular quiet
when music pauses,
the joy in your face
as a dipper skims the river,
that special, transforming second
when a child's wide-awake gaze
is covered in sleep and I watch …

Wordless moments
when everything is stilled
and held life-long in love.

What can a poem do?

(for Irfan and Rabia – to celebrate their marriage)

My words can't keep you
free from all harm
or give you good things.
Life's mistakes and hurts
won't be prevented
by a poem's good wishes.

But words may lift hearts
making it possible, maybe,
to walk from here changed
and challenged.
There must always be stories
and poetry to create the images
we need in our lives:
to tell of flowers
that bloom in the desert;
of birds that sing in a war zone;
of people who love
and go on loving
in the midst of upheaval
and hatred.

We are all made of stories,
and shaped by language.
It is said you lose your soul
if you can't tell your story.
In giving our stories
we care for one another.

In sharing our stories
we preserve our humanity
and know ourselves
fully alive.

Poetry gives us pause
to rejoice in the wonder
and lament the sorrows
of everyday living,
to wander in a garden
gathering the flowers
of thoughts and good wishes;
to nurture and sustain love;
to touch the unknowable heart
of all our living.

Like the flight of a bird
caught in the sunlight
then disappearing
into the trees,
words go free
to make for us all
a touching place.

Let us, with you,
hold the beauty,
the love and diversity,
harmony and joy,

faith and relationship,
blessings and poetry,
of this day.

It's all miracle enough:
this creative, loving power
within which we live and move
and have our being.
Carry its light and beauty
with you every ordinary day.

Let your life together
write the new story
and be the poetry
of what it is to be human,
alive and loving
on this good earth.

Sibyl's poem

This is the story,
the one to live by,
the dream to die with:
curlews call all around,
wild flowers colour the path,
and those you love
walk by your side
to the sea
where the caress of waves
on your wounded body
carries you far from our reach,
far out into the forever
of love and laughter,
of thankfulness and serenity,
of remembering
and resurrection.

Possibilities

There is the myth of creation:
the telling that seeks meaning
and a reason for being

and

then there is new life:
the breath of spring,

the green shoot,
the butterfly wings,
the daffodil burst
and the baby born.

There is the subversive story:
imagination telling it as it is
and how it could be
without any striving
to make sense,
not a Truth
but a pattern.

Healing words?

(for Anne, with love)

Might we gather good memories,
and tell our stories, taking us back
to the day we walked the labyrinth
with the enthusiasm of small children
then paused to smell the hyacinths,
or to that basket filled with apples
you wanted to get closer to,
needing to touch and to smell
the beauty of the fruit,
or maybe the damp morning orchard
with apples sleeping in the grass.

Could other, half-remembered, images
reawaken our sense of wonder:
the woodbrown glow of conkers
before time takes their shine,
leaves shimmering
in the autumn light,
waves rolling timelessly
on so many shores,
known and imagined,
sunflowers that turn each day
to follow the sun,
the depth of knowing
and unknowing in a child's smile,
the delicacy of tiny hands
and the beauty of age-worn hands,
faces of family, friends and strangers,
people extraordinary in their ordinariness,
the bird as it soars and sings
a song that will never save us
but might keep us in touch
with the unknowable.

Then might this poem reach
beyond the sorrow and the anger
to the quiet and reflective heart
of love and beauty,
life … and hope
that is healing.

Geo poet

Don't you like the idea
of a geo-poet –
one who can release
poems from the rocks
that hold our stories,
like Sibelius did with music,
make the poem take form,
the sound hold for a time,
and consciousness keep
the words.

I met a geo-poet once.
He talked of stones,
had one in his pocket
as did I.
We wondered:
What is rock?
What is stone?
What is pebble?

Thought of the rocks
under our feet.
He told me a name I forget
but he made them sing.

Christmas story 2019

Come closer,
I'll tell you a story.
Come, move into the picture,
be enchanted by beauty,
moved by suffering,
surprised by angels
and distant stars.
Draw near to haloes and holiness,
to a straw-filled cradle
and a baby's tiny hands
reaching out
through suffering and joy,
wanting a future.

Come closer
with the quiet people,
the humble ones
who may not inherit the earth
and do it less harm than some.
(The wise men will come later
bringing unsuitable but symbolic gifts,
claiming the light, making history)
Come with the care-givers,
shepherds with lambs,
women with stories to share
and food for the family.

Come closer,
listen and delve deep

into the human
source of the song
Mary, everywoman, sings
to her son and every child
whose eyes open at birth
on to storied light.
Honour littleness
and vulnerability.

Come closer,
you are needed here
to go on telling
this subversive story
born out of
power and oppression,
injustice and fear

but bearing witness
to all that is good and surprising
at the heart of humanity.

Come closer,
the story is for you
and it keeps on growing.
What matters is to wonder,
imagine, discern and trust,
to let each image
tell, pure and unpolluted,
a good story.

Sharing a story

Picture this:
Orkney, summer 1919:
the German High Seas Fleet
held captive in Scapa Flow,
the men on board prisoners,
demoralised, without hope,
hungry for home.

Midsummer Day, 21st June
dawns dry and bright
with clear blue skies
as excited schoolchildren
board *The Flying Kestrel*
for a special day out
to view these ships at anchor.

I might wonder now
about the strange thinking
behind this sightseeing trip
but what the children see
that day is extraordinary
and never to be forgotten.

Their ship is out in the Flow
when the order comes
to scuttle the Fleet
and the ships begin to sink,
and the men scramble for safety
and the greatest single loss

of shipping in maritime history
happens before the eyes
of amazed children.

Some are frightened.
Some are exhilarated.
Some think this a performance
put on especially for them.
One knowing boy turns
to his little sister saying:
'Don't be afraid.
We are witnessing history.'

**

Move on:
to 23rd June 2019:
the story is told again
from the pulpit
of St Magnus Cathedral;
told by a priest
whose uncle was that boy;
whose mother the little girl.

The cathedral stones gather stories,
and today as I sit quietly among them
I too witness history
as we all do, each day
of our lives. Not big events
but stories told in tiny moments
like this one: how the horror

of that day in 1919
becomes strangely beautiful
in a mind-blowing,
heart-stopping moment:
when during morning worship
I share the peace
with two German naval officers

And pause to wonder what voice
might a poet best inhabit
to tell this story,
to hold the memories,
my own and others',
and trust the future:
an ongoing promise
to our Europe,
to our world.

Note: After the German surrender in November 1918 the German High Seas Fleet was held at Scapa Flow in Orkney. Orders were passed by the German High Command to scuttle the fleet on 21st June 1919 – a momentous event witnessed quite by chance by a visiting group of schoolchildren! I was in St Magnus Cathedral in June 2019.

Prisoner

(for Behrouz Boochani)

Around the jagged edge of silence:
poems, stories, images …
waiting without pattern.

A pause on the edge:
words out there –
somewhere.
The one thing necessary
glittering just out of reach,
waiting to be drawn in
to each quiet moment.
The dark silence
contemplated
gives more light
and sound
to the wild rose
rambling the hedgerows,
to the water running over
rocks, pooling and reflecting,
to the distant mountains
blue with hope,
and the waves blessing
the seashore
where a child waits,
where a sea-washed stone
that is what it is, silently,
may fit perfectly

into open human hands
holding its question.

The tears flow,
enough to flood our dreams;
yet beauty heals

and the caged bird of silence
is still there
waiting to be free …

Note: In 2013 Kurdish journalist Behrouz Boochani sought asylum in Australia but was instead illegally imprisoned in the country's most notorious detention centre on Manus Island where he spent six years, eventually being released to New Zealand in November 2019. This poem was written to be part of a book of letters, messages etc made for him by my friend Alison Phipps and presented to him as part of a low-key 'in conversation' public event in NewZealand. If you'd like to know more, I recommend Behrouz's book No Friend but the Mountains.

From within the dark times

I sense the intensity of each moment
and reach for the present hope
in words and poetry.
Why write poems? Why read?
Might the words extend the space,
create a place where sorrow and pain
are shared and everyday joy lived fully?
Might poems express the chaos within
necessary to give birth to the dancing star?

The world's best arguments
won't change a mind.
Only poetry, or a good story,
will do that.

So my poem strives not to belittle
your power of thought
but to expand your spirit
and show the depth, variety
and richness of life.
It reaches for the inexpressible
unique human being that is you.

The fragile hope of survival
lies in how we see,
how we live one with another,
how we recognise the unknowable,
and live with uncertainties,
how we honour the Earth

our mother and sustainer.
As we struggle
in bewilderment
new leaves open
on birch and hawthorn,
bluebells carpet our woodlands,
and birds sing to the dawn

and we know
that there will be a future.
How we see it,
what we hope for, is
and can only ever be
in our own hands.
It's in our love.
It's in our poetry.
For now, in this place
to be here is all,
like the cellist I heard once
at the Bay of Skaill,
rejoicing in the place
and the moment,
playing into the bird song
and sea sounds.

Or remembering the wonder
of hearing that gentle scraping
uncovering 3000 years,

in the Ness of Brodgar,
sounding a story,
the detail of a place.
Watch, hear, absorb,
hold each sacred moment.
Here, now.

More than human wisdom,
looking is the poet's charge:
to mark and mourn
death and loss;
to not let things go by
unnoticed; to respond
to the daily miracles, the music
of wind in the trees,
across stones, in the grass,
the shimmer of the willow –

how I see your face
in the darkness of absence.

April, 2020

This poem has also appeared in Voices Out of Lockdown *edited by Jan Sutch Pickard, published by Wild Goose Publications, 2020.*

Seashore thoughts

Revelations and reflections,
memories and imaginings,
shadowy echoes, ebbing and flowing,
sea sounds, ripples and splashes,
wind over stones, over waving grass,
fragile as coral and fine shells,
sandy as summer feet:
the shore is a musical place.

I hear the water lap
against the rotting wood
of the old boat of history
left high and dry
and slowly disintegrating
with passing time.
It's more weather-beaten
by the day but still there,
where imagination becomes all
of heaven and recollections
held in the senses,
felt on the body,
for always, beyond
consciousness, where light
might outshine itself
and by grace return
as a thought catches it.

One day I may lie down again
on a rocky shore and create

dreams. The best one
will be where I am fully alive
and can name this longing
for the wind's touch,
the sound of water
and the light
of the seashore.

So much

is about touch
and what it is
not: to be in touch
is not touching
and yet for now
it is a non-risk all.

With my hands
around a mug of tea
there is the sensation
of comfort, of home,
but I am disturbed
by weeping I can't hear
and hands that reach out
but can't touch.

Summer 2020

In the absence of the Festival*

Orkney – Midsummer:
salt taste in the wind,
sea sounds hanging
on a stave of light.
In memoried moments
I walk the shore,
tuned to the poetry
and the music
of many dreams.

Somewhere deep inside me
a curlew calls and a cellist plays
in the Atlantic wind
of The Bay of Skaill.
A marimba sounds through a garden,
a blackbird sings with a violin
and a flute is backed by the sea.

In a time without touch
so many sensations
are held in memory:
ebbing and flowing sea,
wind over stones,
around corners of buildings,
over waving grass, across sand.
Music on the shore mingles
with music in concert halls.

I'm savouring past sounds
as Wordsworth, homebound,
rejoiced in the Lakeland daffodils.

Moments never forgotten but held
in the heart to feed the intellect
in dark times. Thought wanders
free and imagination opens me
to some understanding of place
and art, closing the space
between here
and there.

Note: The St Magnus Festival is held at Midsummer every year in Orkney. Ian and I have supported it for over 20 years and I was asked to write this for the year the live Festival didn't happen.

Imagine time ...

to think,
that most under-rated,
essential, entirely deceptive
of activities;

to look and say
what we see
with the fire of poetry;
to light up the mind
with a word on the wind;

to burn the rhetoric
and excite the politics
with the wonder
of story
and the challenge
of beauty.

Fearing illness

Dementia: to lose
memory, mind, being
and soul. Most feared
of illnesses (for what am I
without my memories?)
until now, maybe,
when to die a statistic
in a pandemic,
an avoidable number,
amid protective suits
and masks, alone,
takes root in my mind
as a dreaded possibility.

A distanced hug

Warmth of a small body,
touch of tiny hands,
the remembered forever
unique top-of-the-head smell,
softness of skin, sounds of quiet joy:

the immensity
of an anticipated
moment of contact,
suspended in stone,
for always.

Summer 2020

Note: This poem was inspired by Dominic Benhura's beautiful sculpture: Joy.

Dominic Benhura is one of the Chapungu Sculptors from Zimbabwe. I took a photograph of the sculpture during a visit to an exhibition at Waterperry Gardens, Oxford but unfortunately we have been unable to make contact with Dominic Benhura to ask for permission to reproduce my photograph.

I am sorry that I'm not able to give a visual introduction to Dominic Benhura's beautiful art but there are many websites which display it very well. Readers might like to search his name and spend an enjoyable time exploring his work.

How to fillet a herring in Hertfordshire

From Watford market my mother
brings home wrapped in newspaper
an unconscious remembering:
sounds of the cold North Sea,
salt, grey smell of the waves,
summer sea days when she was young
and herring plentiful in Norfolk
where she belongs and I,
child of the Home Counties,
am a stranger still.

Many times, I watch
her in the kitchen,
see that swift movement
over the fish with skill
as good as any fishwife
in 1940s' Yarmouth.

Now in my remembering
it all becomes something like
a Wordsworth ballad:
the life and language
of ordinary people,
the activities and the dialect
that made an authentic voice:

hers and a little bit mine
in the way I knew
until I went to school,
dodman not snail
bishy barnabee not ladybird.

The iambic voice: her rhythm
and movement first known
with no choice
and like the filleting of fish
staying with me.

Queues

are different now

There's no waiting room
with shifting feet, nervous hands
and occasional smiles of reassurance.

Just a disembodied voice saying
I am number three in a queue.
I wait, imagining number two:
maybe a worried mother
holding a sickly child
or I picture number one
speaking to a kindly nurse
of an elderly mother
who could be dying.

And stretching out invisibly
so many more
with their own stories
listening for the voice
that tells the queue
is getting shorter.

Faceless, distanced,
yet together we wait

like all the invisible dying
who appear as numbers every day.

Queues are different now.

Wintersong

Cold air comes from the sea
across darkened fields,
bidding the trees rest,
quieting their heartbeat.
Time slows and days shorten.
Silently in the soil
the colours of spring
wait for the lengthening light.
All things hold, still and cold.

We value light hoarded
from summer days –
the little light
the moth knows
and the fox pauses in,
natural light of moon,
of stars and guttering candles –
that helps us love
the winter dark.

Now is the time:
bring in the winter leaves
and the winter scents,
share stories, books and music.
Hunker down in the long moments.
Then light the tree with Christmas love
to bless this winter stillness,
to celebrate the season's promise.

Catch a spark …

As the match girls did
in long-ago London,
saving themselves,
holding the light.

Catch a spark
as a poet did
holding the words
to shape the story,
to light the flow.

Catch a spark
as the composer did
with soul and sound;
a work beyond words
to include us all.

Catch a spark
in homes and hovels,
refuges and refugee camps,
prisons and palaces,
Listen: for voices
and violins
Let the spirit
go free, the soul rejoice
in humanity and hope.

Catch a spark
of human creativity,
the inclusive language
of community,
the irrepressible rhythm
of the Earth,
the music of consciousness
to awaken and heal
us all.

Catch a spark.
See it, hear it, hold it
until …

Note: This poem is inspired by the Lampades of Greek mythology; the match girls' strike of 1888; 'The Spark Catchers', a poem by Lemn Sissay which first appeared in Gold from the Stone, Canongate, 2016; *and a musical composition by Hannah Kendall with the same title.*

First morning

Lockdown 2

For a minute happiness came
pure and immediate.
I stepped outside into winter sun,
a little warmth on my back
and in the air a huge silence.
A beautiful 'I don't know'
out of which some good
will one day surely come.

Lockdown 3

Maybe it's only in winter's pause
when everyone's gone indoors,
the planes have stopped flying,
the cars quietly parked
that we listen wholly
to what the Earth is saying.

2021

Blessings

A quiet unassuming day
light morning sun,
gentle breezes and kindly rain
caress a tired garden.

Hope surfaces
in shoots of green,
tiny, barely noticeable.

Then all at once
an outburst of little birds –
long-tailed tits, wrens,
blue tits, great tits –
descends to celebrate
the coming of the rain
in the refreshed birdbath
and the day over-runs
with joy.

?

So many answers
but if I peel away
the fatuous reasoning,
like the layers of an onion,
will I find at the heart
the wrong question?

As the poet more or less said
we humans are not able
to take too much reality
but now must be the time
to look hard
for challenging,
compassionate questions
worthy of our humanity.

A breath of fresh air

The virus and death
in the air, everywhere.

Yet in a brief moment
of sun, I breathe freely,
breathe in birdsong
and earth scents.

I try to be conscious
of what it is I do,
as I breathe in
the joy of being
of grass and leaf
of winter rain
and saturated earth,
the tree smell of home.

I watch the moment,
how the air enters
and leaves my body.
I'm taking time to celebrate
each breath as it moves
into the wonder of memory:
'What of this moment
 do I want to remember?'

I breathe out the books
I've read, the words,
the music I've heard,
the love lived every day.

Here … or … there,
in … or … out,
in this moment
of conscious celebration
breath is prayer.

February 2021

What if …

we all tell our stories
of suffering and pain,
of hope and new life.
Not polemic but poetry,
not protest **against**
(we know what is wrong)
but words speaking **for**,
stories of who I am
and who you are,
beautifully and gently told.

What if …
our lives speak the best
of what it is to be alive,
what it is to be human,
to discern those things
that are noble, good,
free of greed, self-interest,

and that most unattractive
of human characteristics:
certainty.

What if …
we attempt to reach our full potential
as compassionate human beings
in true and equal relationship
with all living things.

What if …
we burn the rhetoric
and excite the politics,
resist all that would destroy
the wonder of imagination
and the challenge of beauty.

What if …
we fully value the ordinary,
the little things:
first flowers of spring,
birds that sing of things
beyond our knowing,
sounds of happy children
with space to run and play,
the smile of an old woman,
watching, laughing, remembering,
everyone fully alive.

What if …
strangers from afar

are welcomed as friends
for the joy they bring.

What if …
we begin to understand
the power of empathy
as imagination with discipline
and commitment
and pass each day
loving not hating.
Would that tell
in our tears
and our smiles?

What if …
against all odds
we go on dreaming
a wild, green world,
equal, fair and just, connected,
with less noise and fewer machines,
where people, less anxious and stressed,
time-rich and happy, bake bread
and share it, grow vegetables together,
where life is sacred and precious
and there's work for hands to do.

What if …
all food shared
with friends and strangers
is valued deeply

and experienced
as a eucharistic meal.

What if …
we uncover the good questions
hidden in fatuous answers
and refuse to stop
asking those questions.

What if …
we believe in people
not markets and pay attention
to what really happens.
Might we then see and value
the creativity, innovation
and hard work of people
whose greatest desire
is to serve others.

What if …
together we contemplate
our beautiful dream
and begin to see
possibilities.

What if …
the fire of poetry and story
reveals deep in our culture
a longing to begin a change
and make it impossible
to return to the world unbothered.

What if …
the longing is strong enough
to make that change inevitable.

What if …

This meditation on imagination, poetry and the possibility of change has also been published separately as a WGP download.

Spring

It's been said before
by me and others:
in spite of the horror
it's all so very beautiful.

Beyond the daffodils
and emerging primroses,
a small broken rainbow,
a tiny 'yes' of hope
like light in the eyes
of a newborn child
or that moment
when the life light
goes out of this world
into eternal peace.

Out of the nothing
all things springing.

Against certainty

I have become old.
This surprises me.
One day I may be
a wise woman
with some answers
… or maybe not:
age, history has shown,
comes with no guarantee
of wisdom.

I feel there's little time left
and the secret, if there is one,
might be to acknowledge
what I can't know,
for isn't 'I don't know'
the beginning of creativity?

Art is the telling, the holding
with respect and amazement
each breathing moment
I am alive.

See: the mighty wings
on which the words
'I don't know' fly high
and low, near and far,
to the inner place
and to all the ends
of the Earth, far, far away

from all I might be told
which is never enough.
There's always more.
Inspiration begins
not from 'I know'
but from 'I don't know'
and ends in a breath
of fresh air.

At my mother's knee ...

I wish I could tell her now
how often I watched, unknowing
yet with every passing moment
learning how it's done:

> folding of shirts,
> filleting of fish,
> bottling of fruit;
> using every last scrap
> of precious food;
> avoiding all waste.

Then at quieter times,
long summer evenings:

> knitting and sewing,
> unravelling the jumpers,
> re-knitting the wool.

Working on the tissue
of paper patterns,
dreaming the dresses,
handling the scissors,
deftly.

And always, the care, the cleaning, the love
that made home a good place.

In the end
to these I return.
They are what created
the basic pattern
for my life.

Letters

A beginner
with a simple pen
and an old ink well
sunk in a worn desk.

Concentration is intense.
My small hand moves
across the page,
making the shapes,

keeping little letters
within central blue lines,
letting the big ones go free
to leap and play
but making sure they loop
just right.

The deep glossiness
and beetle sparkle
of ink creeps
along the line,
wanting no blots
to mar perfection.

The artistry of it all:
the possibility of learning,
the beauty of connection,
the means to tell
a story to the future,
to a world unknown
and unknowing.

Passport …

… unused, whispers
where I didn't go,
and where I am,
where I belong
and what it is to be
fully here: a place to stay
with quiet but active mind
and steady feet.

No wandering to 'there'
to discover the 'wild',
knowing 'wild' is here
and everywhere.
Nature is living wilderness
whether meadow or moor,
patch of earth, green shoot,
virus or hurricane,
shady tree or running water.
It's where
I am …

… ready to till a little soil,
to plant and grow,
to bake bread;
to welcome wholly
friend and stranger,
love always.
Wild is where we are,
our home: a holy place.

Awake!

Be gentle as you walk
on the good Earth,
our home and life-giver.
Touch with kindness
all that has being
and shares with you
this sacred space.

Be still and connect
in the silence
what you are
with what you value.

Give attention to life's littleness.
Contemplate what it means
to honour the small things –
the seeds and sunlight –
that sustain our wider being.
Listen, feel, touch and smell;
think and imagine –
these are sacred acts.
Real life is what it is,
not what you might be told it is.

Watch and never turn away.
Discern what is needful.
We can no longer sleep unaware
nor be silent while others sleep.
May the sound of our own voices
disturb our foolish slumber.

Awake and see!
Awake and tell what you see!
Awake and seek
a beautiful future
for all the Earth
and its creatures.

A fuller version of this has been published as a Wild Goose Publications digital down-load: Nature, Life and Being.

To find a home in the world

that's the holy grail.

To know home
is to be at one
with all that lives,
to discover an earthing
and grounding place,
neither here
nor elsewhere,
neither separation
nor connection,
solitude without loneliness,
present with possibilities
for peace or for conflict.

To know home
is to honour a sacred place
with its own rituals
and rites of being.
To write is a searching
for home.

Home is
to share life's moments.
It's a library: the one or two
well worn books treasured
or the many that tell
a life.

'Homely' he said
'I like it' –
my friend who was born
in Pakistan talking
of what we might think
to be my home.
Himself at home
here, being himself,
balancing difference.

To know home
is to reimagine
them and us,
here and there.
Our stories are home
and yet surprise us
with strangeness.

At dusk the children
are called in from play,
in from the dark,
into the dream language
of home.

Translation

Of all the strange thoughts to wake me
at night, possibly the strangest
is the need to get ready, to prepare,
for something as yet unknown.

One day the strangeness, fear even,
will be gone and all will be in order.
In imagination, I will go from here
across a dreamed-of meadow
of larks and sweet grass,
to the longed-for sea
and beyond, contemplating
who I have become
and what translation
of a language and being
that is mine alone
will be left
when I've gone.

Thanks for the memory

In the dark times
I look back for a while,
contemplate my life
in its unfailing wonder,
remember, imagine, dream,
see the past laid before me
in images of bewitching beauty
and devastating heartbreak.

I see again
in the eye of my mind
that sunlit path
to sand and sea
where once I danced
with friends;
and enjoy once more
from the quiet of my heart
the way winter sun
gilds bare trees
and the morning glow
promises a good day;
and brings to mind
a newspaper photograph,
an unforgettable image:
of children seesawing
either side of the wall
that attempts to divide them.

I cherish with gratitude
the gentle hopes embedded
in such fragile moments
and am nourished.

Beauty is to be savoured,
the salt of our being,
alongside all the fears, tears
and contradictions.
Poetry juggles it all
into a liveable space for now
and a vision for the future.

2021

Our gate

There's a gate in our garden
not far from the house.
Squirrels run along the top.
Birds use it to rest a while.

This gate keeps nobody in or out.
I can easily pass through
into the refreshing world of the field
and the smell of summer grass,
greener maybe on this side.
Sounds are reassuring:
bees, grasshoppers, birds
working at their own survival.

There's a feeling of freedom;
the air seems strangely different
on this side of the gate.
Breathing is easier, the light
greater: I can see distant hills.

The gate is a place of pause,
a way through to an opportunity:
maybe a chance to sit in the sun
with a rug, a friend, tea and cake,
to dream of larks and wild flowers
to come, maybe, in their own time
with a sense of completeness
like finding the words
to make a story
and shape a poem.

Doubt … and trust

How strange to doubt:
to plant the seed and not see
an image of the flower in bloom.
How strange to think maybe
it won't grow, and so to wait
and wait, and lose all hope.
Then what joy: a shoot, a leaf,
the bloom of flowers – a gift
to dissolve all doubt
to sustain and nurture
faith and hope.

The funeral

The funeral service
felt strange to them.
They talked each to each
of the 'religious bit'
now thankfully over.

But with familiar food
to prepare and share,
sandwiches and fruit cake
to hand around
to friend and stranger,
came a familiarity,
a wordless communion,
opening all to something
relevant and significant:
'Come, and share.'

Very short stories

Love

I see you still
in the old man
disguise.

My life

I wonder, when I die
will my hands be clenched
and if so what will I hold
within them.

Herstory

After he died
the garden he loved
and controlled
became her place
and she began
to understand
resurrection.

Across water

To live on an island
is the comfort
of knowing boundaries
and poetry that connects
beyond borders.

One day

On your birthday
the tree creepers we saw
in Henry Moore's Garden
made a small memory
in a skyline
of momentous art forms.

My language

Everything I write begins
with impetus and feeling,
notion, impulse and imagination,
then becomes the thing itself,
translation being at the heart
of all things.

Golden eagle

Wild was close
in those few seconds
it took for the huge bird
to emerge from behind a rock,
fly across her path
almost touching her small body,
her three years of life on Earth,
connecting two beings,
one planet.

Rust

What is the story light tells
as rust comes
from a nowhere place
and the shape of the past
is transformed.

A wild rose grows over
a tin roof and beneath
the fleeting flowers
is a hint of rust, writing
its own momentary story.
A tree forces its way through
the rusted remains
of an abandoned tractor;
machinery left in the field
turns rich orange-gold
in its cloak of green;
a red-rust vehicle axle
sinks into the sands of time
on a distant seashore.

What is the story light tells
as time makes of discarded metal
the poetry of something other:
an elemental beauty, fiery,
sharp with acidic scents
and flushed with decay.

Rust challenges certainty,
and sureness of form,
disintegrating solidity
into randomness,
a process, something
on the way, returning,
as all things must,
to a rust-red universe;
something turning
to no thing.

Note: This poem was inspired by Stephen Raw's book of photographs: Where
Ferrous Metal Meets Air and Water *published by Rust Books and Carcanet
Press, 2021) and* Rust: The Art Gallery *('the sole function of which is to cele-
brate the texture, sculpture and colour of rust').*

The way through

Gates, doors, stiles,
go-through places,
doorsteps and doorways,
edges: I love the space
these create in my mind,
the connections revealed
and stories waiting.

I might follow light
into the just visible,

into the mystery,
through partly open doors
to the inner sanctuary
of garden sheds and little dens
or maybe through an arch,
anticipating the unlikely beyond.
I might pause
on a threshold,
not to venture in,
but to wonder
at a spirit-filled space
in an empty church.

Dappled light
through fretwork gates
patterns a pathway;
a candle flickers
in a window
giving a little light
and many shadows;
coloured light
through stained glass
makes a carpet
on stone flags.

And so the light opens
for a slowly passing stranger
an imaginative window
on to something
as yet unthought.

Jug

I remember
a rusted enamel jug,
abandoned, no longer useful,
beside an empty cottage,
no one around to tell
its story. Its meaning
now in its being:
a form out of reach
of Keats' wild ecstasy.
But there is truth here,
something we need
to know of beauty:
not leaf-tinged legend,
nor attic shape but everyday
ordinariness, of soil and rooting
where once water poured.

It's an accidental artwork,
impermanent. Orange rust
speaks decay and teases
not out of thought
but out of being

and beauty endures
because
I remember.

A last conversation

(For Anne with love)

Shadows it seems will find a way
to creep through the light
as around a lamp
on an unfamiliar road.
But it's not the darkness
we need to understand.
It's the light; not death
but the life you have known
in the fullness of being
and the goodness of people;
the beauty you have given
and the compassion shown.
As I take your hand now
suddenly there is a clarity
beyond any search for meaning:
the darkness and the light
being much the same.

The silence, the unspoken words,
hold a peace beyond our knowing
and from the depths of being
I hear a whisper:
'Remember me.'

Then, I see how it will be, this light,
this life-and-death understanding.
In each stone I pick up

I will look for the blue
that delighted you;
in each tiny flower
I will see the delicacy
that entranced you;
and when the conkers
fall again on the road
to the Meeting House
I will remember
how we filled our pockets
with their shining, all the time
knowing they would fade.
I will wonder at the poetry
of each remembered moment,
at the pattern of small things
and the joy of resurrection.

August 2021

Shelf-life

Stones and cones,
sea glass and shells,
odd-shaped wood
and broken pots,
things picked up
along the way:
all have many shades
of silence and stories
rarely told.

Such things survive
by chance and in memory:
hand-held or as moments
the mind holds: retrieved
as unexhausted fragments.

Attention fully paid
to object, person, place,
lives on, translated
to words and ways,
stories to live by,
being and things glorified
just because they are.

Into the story

An owl flies across the moon:
in Israel, Palestine or Jordan
where farmers and shepherds
join hands in peace
to protect this wise bird,
their friend and helper
in working and living well.*

An owl flies across the moon:
into the dreamtimes. An old, old story
tells of a stable in Bethlehem town,
a child in a manger and shepherds abiding.
On wings of wisdom and imagination
the owl, mostly unseen and untold,
flies with the angels this Christmas night
as free as the ongoing promise
of peace and goodwill for all the earth.

An owl flies across the moon:
as people cry, as people laugh,
and stories go on evolving.
Imagination is making things happen
but nothing is unravelled
to its core. Stories we live by
will never be fully told.
But we will go on risking delight,
cultivating beauty, creating colour
and nurturing wonder.

An owl flies across the moon:
an image of hope
in stories yet to be told.

Christmas 2021

* In a partnership begun many years ago Palestinian, Israeli and Jordanian farmers work with scientists and ornithologists to encourage owls as a sustainable way to control rats and mice.

Biblical references:

Micah 1:8
That is why I lament and wail,
Despoiled and naked;
I howl like a wolf, mourn like a
desert owl.

Isaiah 34:10,11
… it will lie waste, and no one will ever again pass through it.
Horned owl and bustard will make it their home; ….

Psalm 102:6
I am like a desert owl in the wilderness

Leviticus 11:17
… they must not be eaten …
the tawny-owl, the fisher-owl, the long-eared owl …

Today

War in Ukraine.
Today's image:*
a father sits slumped
beside a hospital trolley,
head in hands. He weeps
into a bloodied cloth
covering the body
of his teenage son.

Personal distress,
one man's private despair,
yet a deeply political
portrayal of the cost
of senseless war.
It's far away yet as close
to me as my understanding
of my own humanity.

Here, now and somewhere else
I cradle the horror of that image
as I gaze, bewildered and helpless,
at the sunlight caressing
a vase of sticky buds
I gathered from a fallen tree
wanting to nurture
their potential for life.
They are beginning to open.
There is a vision, amen maybe,
or a question forming deep

down in the dearest freshness.
And an answer:
something like hope,
that the buds' dying beauty
might challenge hatred
with something like healing.

* The image/photograph was on the front page of The Guardian, *3rd March, 2022.*

Searching

(For Michael and family and in memory of Anne)

We are looking for you.
We gather words and images,
the things you treasured,
so many unnamed delights
and life-changing thoughts.
We read and reflect. We talk
but most of all we wonder
that after we have gathered
each small thing,
every last word,
what we have remains
incomplete.
We will never hold
or tell the essence,
the wholeness

that is you.
The spirit will always go free
beyond the reach of our knowing.

The words and images
will fade. Our thoughts
and memories will settle
like a fine dust
over all things
and we will be left
with the inexpressible:
a great silence,
a great darkness
and the beauty
of one small light
continuing to shine.

October 2021

Grief

Awareness
strangely heightened;
how fragile the world is,
as delicate as a tiny flower
not least in connections,
where humanity is felt:
    the gentle young man who pauses
    to talk, distanced, on a footpath,
    the child who runs after a pushchair
    returning a toddler's dropped toy,
    the reassuring receptionist,
    volunteer or shop assistant,
    silly outdoor fun with family
    and old friends,
    a wave, a smile, lighting a candle,
    reading a poem, playing music.
All encounters and actions
of ordinary people
who don't attempt to explain
loss or try to work it out
by some strange philosophy
or mysterious belief of their own.
They reveal blessings to be counted
and a quietness that is life going on.

Nearness of others,
of things, matters
and lets me *be*.

Going

I am walking where the winds blow
patterns in red and gold
feeling the year growing old.
Leaves drenched with sunsets show
a year's lifeblood on every tree
and memories the summer made
lighten every autumn shade.
Thoughts are fallen leaves, blowing free.
Autumn is fragile; it has its own grief.
We learn to love and let go,
find strength to walk away, to know
a breaking but not to clasp each leaf
as it falls. There is an ease
in letting go that brings in peace.

On consolation

When a friend dies
part of me is lost.
In the darkness:
flowers, books, stones, colour,
music, pictures ... cake
and conversations ...
losing a little light.

Where are you
who loved life, adventure
talked of living fully,
dancing through each day
hand in warm hand?

But not now …
no point saying 'I miss you'
and there are no words
to come near
what you were.

Now you are nowhere
… and everywhere.

Distancing

The path from you to me suffers little
from lack of use. I could walk there today
and know the strangeness would be nothing more
than a few dead leaves blown along the way.

Clothes shopping in Colonsay

(for Jan, with love)

A small island bathed in sunshine,
tea in a flower-filled garden
alive with birdsong and bee sound.
The setting is perfect.

Getting on for 50 years' friendship
and today is a first. We're doing
what women do, or so it is said,
trying on clothes, admiring
each other in possible purchases:
yours for a wedding, serious choosing.
Me, unusually, I'm just playing
and relishing something so different
in our long friendship; a moment
not to be forgotten, probably
never to be repeated.

Small matter maybe, but significant.
More so as we grow older. It is said
the gods make their own importance,
and the muse will come unsummoned
to the ordinary moment as today maybe
with an unexpected resurgence of delight.

Reading Sappho*

Fragments.
Just papyrus scraps
holding on to words,
loose and wandering
amid fragility of materials,
and the pattern of decay.

Wonder at their survival
and something like rebirth.
It's all a challenge
to certainty;
a light held up
to the imagination
long after rust
has returned
metal to earth,
guns to ground.

Connect with one poet
of the past. Reach out
from the edges
into what is missing
as if to taste, touch and feel,
to breathe in something
from the empty spaces
where from the words
that might have been
and the words that remain
we sense the hesitation of history
and the complexity of poetry.

* Sappho lived on the island of Lesbos around 630 BC. Her writing – now just beautiful fragments – is the earliest poetry we know to have been written by a woman.

Now you have gone …

(For Sheila)

Now you have gone
my friend who loved flowers
each bloom I hold
ready for a vase,
seems to tell of you.
I imagine your touch and smile,
that moved each one of us
with wholeness, faith and love
as given to a well-tended garden:
down-to-earth and colourful.
You shared another's suffering
and your tears would fall
like gentle rain, nurturing,
renewing, reviving.
You delighted in another's joy
and your face would glow
like a sunflower
turning to the sun.

Now you have gone
I remember how you loved
the trees that reach out

across a country lane,
meeting at the centre
and how in a similar way
your welcoming hands
reached out to others
in unfailing friendship.
You offered the comfort
of the ordinary: conversation,
with tea and food to share
and that un-ordinary extra,
the inexpressible gift
that came from the heart
of all that was you.

October 2021

Making poems

At the end of the day
gather like treasures
each smile that beams
from a stranger,
each experience and encounter,
each colour and sound,
word and understanding.
Consider each petal that falls
from a rose,
or raindrop
from a leaf.
Turn them over
in your mind.
Touch, smell, look, consider,
breathe each one.
Know it to be irreplaceable.
Then place, draw,
write and settle it.
Trace the lines of its being.
Make it live
for always.